W9-CHQ-954

INSIDE THE
NFL

NEW ORLEANS
SAINTS

BY WILLIAM MEIER

SportsZone

An Imprint of Abdo Publishing
abdobooks.com

abdobooks.com

Published by Abdo Publishing, a division of ABDO, PO Box 398166, Minneapolis, Minnesota 55439. Copyright © 2020 by Abdo Consulting Group, Inc. International copyrights reserved in all countries. No part of this book may be reproduced in any form without written permission from the publisher. SportsZone™ is a trademark and logo of Abdo Publishing.

Printed in the United States of America, North Mankato, Minnesota
042019
092019

Cover Photo: Aaron M. Sprecher/AP Images
Interior Photos: Paul Sancya/AP Images, 5; David J. Phillip/AP Images, 7, 10; Mike Groll/AP Images, 9; Focus on Sport/Getty Images, 13, 19; Jack Thornell/AP Images, 15; JRT/AP Images, 17; AP Images, 21; Al Messerschmidt/AP Images, 23; NFL Photos/AP Images, 25; Bill Feig/AP Images, 26, 43; James A. Finley/AP Images, 28; Eric Gay/AP Images, 31, 35; Dave Martin/AP Images, 32; Butch Dill/AP Images, 37; Greg Trott/AP Images, 39; Gerald Herbert/AP Images, 41

Editor: Patrick Donnelly
Series Designer: Craig Hinton

Library of Congress Control Number: 2018965646

Publisher's Cataloging-in-Publication Data

Names: Meier, William, author.
Title: New Orleans Saints / by William Meier
Description: Minneapolis, Minnesota: Abdo Publishing, 2020 | Series: Inside the NFL | Includes online resources and index.
Identifiers: ISBN 9781532118586 (lib. bdg.) | ISBN 9781532172762 (ebook) | ISBN 9781644941126 (pbk.)
Subjects: LCSH: New Orleans Saints (Football team)--Juvenile literature. | National Football League--Juvenile literature. | Football teams--Juvenile literature. | American football--Juvenile literature.
Classification: DDC 796.33264--dc23

TABLE OF CONTENTS

CHAPTER 1

SAINTS MARCH TO THE TOP

Sean Payton held the Lombardi Trophy high in the air. Then he turned and handed it to Drew Brees. Payton was the head coach of the New Orleans Saints. Brees was the team's quarterback. They hugged. Brees planted a kiss on the trophy. It was a moment that Saints fans thought might never take place.

On February 7, 2010, Brees and Payton led New Orleans to its first Super Bowl victory. The Saints beat the Indianapolis Colts 31–17 in Super Bowl XLIV in Miami, Florida. The victory put an end to a 43-year quest to be the best in the National Football League (NFL).

"We just believed in ourselves," Brees said moments after receiving the trophy. "We knew that we had an entire city

Quarterback Drew Brees proudly lifts the Lombardi Trophy after the Saints defeated the Indianapolis Colts.

GETTING THEIR CHANCE

Before the 2009 season, 27 of the NFL's 32 teams had been to the Super Bowl at least once. The Saints made their first Super Bowl appearance that season. Through the 2018 season, just four NFL teams still had never played in the Super Bowl: the Cleveland Browns, the Detroit Lions, the Houston Texans, and the Jacksonville Jaguars.

and maybe even an entire country behind us. I've tried to imagine what this moment would be like for a long time, and it's even better than expected."

Winning the Super Bowl is a major accomplishment for any football team. But the win was bigger than that for many people in New Orleans, Louisiana. The city had been devastated by Hurricane Katrina in 2005. The hurricane destroyed much of the city and many people died as a result.

The storm caused severe damage to the Saints' home stadium, the Louisiana Superdome. Thousands of locals had to use the stadium for shelter after their homes were destroyed. Although many people left the city, the Saints stayed.

The Saints always had a strong following in New Orleans throughout their 43 mostly losing seasons. After Hurricane Katrina, that bond grew. The Saints helped bring the city together after it was torn apart by the natural disaster.

The Louisiana Superdome was severely damaged by Hurricane Katrina. Locals used it as a shelter.

"People have asked me so many times, 'Do you look at it as a burden or extra pressure? Do you feel like you're carrying the weight of the city on your team's shoulders?'" Brees said of playing quarterback for the Saints. "I said, 'No, not at all.' We all

COOL BREES

The 2009 season was Drew Brees's ninth in the NFL and his fourth with the Saints. He began his career by playing five seasons with the San Diego Chargers. Brees signed a six-year contract with New Orleans in 2006. He quickly picked up where he left off as one of the NFL's best quarterbacks. He threw 122 touchdown passes in his first four seasons with the Saints. Brees also made the Pro Bowl three times and was named the NFL's Offensive Player of the Year in 2008.

Brees earned fans in New Orleans for his efforts off the field, too. After moving there, he embraced the city in a way that few professional athletes do. Brees became active in local charities. He also helped raise money to help those in need in the hurricane-battered city. Brees said the impact he has had on the city has matched the impact the city has had on him and the Saints.

look at it as a responsibility. Our city, our fans give us strength. We owe this to them. That's made all the difference.

"There's no city, there's no organization, there's no people that we would want to win more for than the city of New Orleans. It's an honor and just an unbelievable feeling."

Brees was voted the Most Valuable Player (MVP) of Super Bowl XLIV. He completed 32 of 39 passes for 288 yards and two touchdowns in the game. As good as Brees was that day, it was Tracy Porter who made the play Saints fans will remember.

Cornerback Tracy Porter celebrates as he heads to the end zone after intercepting Peyton Manning's pass in the fourth quarter of Super Bowl XLIV.

The Saints had a 24–17 lead late in the game. But the Colts had the ball. Their quarterback, Peyton Manning, had won his fourth league MVP award that season. Now he was guiding the Colts down the field in search of a game-tying touchdown.

✕ Saints head coach Sean Payton celebrates after winning Super Bowl XLIV.

But before the Colts could reach the end zone, Manning threw an ill-advised pass. Porter picked it off and ran 74 yards for a touchdown. That gave New Orleans a 31–17 lead. The Colts could not come back.

"Everything slowed down," Porter said of the play. "The spiral on the ball slowed down. The guys around me slowed down. The crowd noise stopped. It was just me and the football."

After so many years of losing seasons, the Saints were finally recognized as the best football team in the world at the end of the 2009 season.

"We're going to enjoy this for a while," Brees said. "This is something that I think we all deserve to enjoy for a while, and reflect on what it's taken to get to this point, and all that we've been through and all that we've fought so hard to get."

WHO DAT?

Saints fans are known throughout the NFL for their favorite cheer: "Who dat say dey gonna beat dem Saints?" The cheer is often shortened to simply, "Who Dat?" The origin of the phrase is unknown. But during the Saints' Super Bowl season, the team's fans and the NFL debated over who owned the phrase. The league did not want the phrase used on unofficial merchandise. Regardless, it has been a Saints tradition. In 1983, local musician Aaron Neville, a New Orleans native, and local artist Steve Monistere produced a song inspired by the chant. The recording also featured several Saints players.

CHAPTER 2

THE NFL WELCOMES THE SAINTS

Dave Dixon was a New Orleans businessman with a dream to bring an NFL team to the city. New Orleans did not have a major professional sports team in the 1960s. That nearly changed in 1963. Dixon tried to buy the Oakland Raiders of the American Football League (AFL) and move them east. But the sale fell through and the Raiders stayed in Oakland.

The dream finally came true in 1966. On November 1, NFL commissioner Pete Rozelle announced that New Orleans would be given an NFL team starting in 1967. Coincidentally, that day was also the Catholic holiday All Saints' Day.

Dixon worked behind the scenes to secure the franchise. But John W. Mecom Jr. became the team owner and president. On January 9, 1967, the team was given the

Wide receiver Danny Abramowicz was one of the Saints' early stars.

THE FIRST SAINTS

The Saints began building their first roster right away. It started with the expansion draft on February 9, 1967. The Saints selected 42 players from the rosters of the existing NFL teams. They also selected 36 players during the 1967 AFL-NFL Draft. Then they made several trades to bring in veteran players. One of the last players the Saints selected during the AFL-NFL Draft was receiver Danny Abramowicz. He led the NFL with 73 receptions in 1969 and was named to the Saints Hall of Fame in 1988.

The early Saints also featured two players who would later go on to make the Pro Football Hall of Fame. The Saints traded for former Chicago Bears star defensive end Doug Atkins in 1967. He played his final three seasons for the Saints and is known as one of the best defensive ends ever. Fullback Jim Taylor only played his final season for the Saints after playing nine seasons with the Green Bay Packers.

nickname "Saints." The name was adopted from the classic jazz song "When the Saints Go Marching In." New Orleans is widely known for its jazz music.

Fans could not wait to see the Saints. The team sold 20,000 season tickets the first day they went on sale. It sold 33,400 season tickets before the 1967 season began. Now the Saints just had to make sure they gave those fans something good to watch on the field.

The Saints worked to build a winning team before the 1967 season. That included making two big trades. Those trades brought in quarterback Gary Cuozzo and fullback Jim Taylor.

Saints running back Don McCall rounds the corner during a game against the Cleveland Browns at Tulane Stadium in 1967.

Cuozzo had spent four years as a backup to Hall of Fame quarterback Johnny Unitas with the Baltimore Colts. But he had done well when he did play. Taylor was considered the NFL's best fullback during his time with the Green Bay Packers. With those two leading the way, the Saints were hopeful for a good first season.

The Saints won their last five preseason games. They hoped to take that success into the regular season. New Orleans played its first official game on September 17, 1967. The Saints faced the Los Angeles Rams at Tulane Stadium in New Orleans.

More than 80,000 fans packed the stands. Their excitement could not be contained. That was especially true when Taylor was introduced. He was a native of nearby Baton Rouge, Louisiana, and a former Louisiana State University star.

Said linebacker Steve Stonebreaker, "The roar that greeted him was unbelievable and unforgettable. Then came Gilliam's flight. That was a miracle."

Stonebreaker was referring to John Gilliam. The rookie receiver wasted no time making Saints history. On the opening kickoff against the Rams—the very first play of the Saints' first official game—Gilliam took it back 94 yards for a touchdown. Despite that thrilling start, the Saints lost to the Rams 27–13.

The Saints had a talented team. But they had a tough task ahead. Expansion teams don't usually do very well in their

John Gilliam returns the opening kickoff 94 yards during the Saints' first regular season game in 1967.

first seasons. It turned out the Saints were no different. They lost their first seven games and finished 3–11 in 1967.

Life did not get any easier after that. Taylor retired after just one season with the Saints. Cuozzo lost his starting job and was traded after that first season. The Saints went 4–9–1 in 1968. They got a little better in 1969. They finished 5–9 but still had a long way to go. Yet the fans remained loyal even with the struggles, filling Tulane Stadium every week. Coach Tom Fears looked to the future with hope.

"They are real tough competitors," he said of his players. "I've never seen this group quit."

CHAPTER 3

TOUGH TIMES

A new decade did not change the fortunes of the Saints. After winning five games in 1969, the Saints won just twice in 1970. They finished 2–11–1. The lone highlight was kicker Tom Dempsey setting an NFL record with a 63-yard field goal.

The team fired head coach Tom Fears after going 1–5–1 during the first half of the season. Fears had been the team's coach since its first season. He was replaced by J. D. Roberts. Roberts would coach the Saints through the 1972 season.

As much as they tried, the Saints could never find a winning formula during the 1970s. They drafted quarterback Archie Manning with the second pick in the 1971 NFL Draft. Although Manning had become one of the league's top

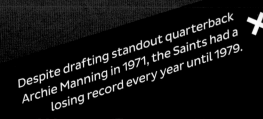

Despite drafting standout quarterback Archie Manning in 1971, the Saints had a losing record every year until 1979.

DEMPSEY'S KICK

The 1970 season was one of the worst in Saints history. But it did have one signature moment. The Saints were hosting the Detroit Lions on November 8 at Tulane Stadium. Detroit led 17–16 as time wound down. On the last play of the game, Saints kicker Tom Dempsey nailed a 63-yard field goal to secure a 19–17 win. It was the longest field goal in NFL history at the time. "I saw the ref with his hands up in the air, and I heard the crowd, and I had to accept the fact that I'd done it," Dempsey said.

Dempsey was born without toes on his right foot. That forced him to wear a special shoe on his kicking foot. Still, Dempsey played 11 NFL seasons. His 63-yard kick held up as the NFL record until December 8, 2013, when Matt Prater of the Denver Broncos converted from 64 yards out. Dempsey only played in New Orleans for the 1969 and 1970 seasons. However, he is a member of the team's Hall of Fame.

quarterbacks, the Saints continued to struggle. They had a losing record every year until 1979. Even then they finished just 8–8. The league had switched to a 16-game season in 1978.

The Saints had six different head coaches throughout the 1970s. One of them was Hall of Famer Hank Stram, who led the Kansas City Chiefs to victory in Super Bowl IV. But even he could not help the Saints. The team finished 7–21 during Stram's two seasons with the club in 1976 and 1977.

Tom Dempsey kicks a 63-yard field goal against the Detroit Lions in 1970. That remained the NFL record until 2013.

The fans had to find things other than winning to get excited about in the 1970s. They had one of those moments in 1975. The Saints moved out of Tulane Stadium after eight years there. They moved into the brand-new Superdome. New Orleans did not have a winning football team, but it supported the Saints. After 1975, they had what was considered the best stadium in pro football. The Superdome seated 69,056 fans.

THE FIRST GREAT MANNING

Archie Manning was the number two pick in the 1971 NFL Draft by the New Orleans Saints. Years later, two of his sons would become first picks in the draft. Peyton Manning was taken first by the Indianapolis Colts in 1998. Eli Manning was taken first overall by the San Diego Chargers in 2004. However, Eli was immediately traded to the New York Giants.

The 1970s were disappointing for most Saints fans. The 1980s did not get off to a much better start. The Saints lost their first 14 games of the 1980 season. Coach Dick Nolan was fired after the twelfth loss. The Saints finished 1–15 that season.

Manning was traded to the Houston Oilers one game into the 1982 season. But the Saints showed signs of improvement in the following years. They matched a team record with eight wins in 1983 and nearly made the playoffs. The Saints needed a win against the Los Angeles Rams in the last game of the regular season to get in. But they ended up losing on a last-second field goal.

The Saints then went back to losing. They won only seven games in 1984 and 1986. They won only five in 1985. By the end of the 1986 season, the Saints had played 20 seasons in the NFL. Yet they had never had a winning record and had never been to the playoffs.

Saints wide receiver Lindsay Scott heads up field after making a catch against the Los Angeles Rams in 1983.

"We were the league's doormats," said Derland Moore, a Saints defensive lineman from 1973 to 1985. "When I went out and people would ask me if I played for the Saints, I would say no."

The fans craved a winner. Manning could only imagine what the city would be like if the Saints were to host a playoff game. He was long gone by the time it happened.

CHAPTER 4

LEARNING TO WIN

It took nine head coaches before the Saints found one who could lead them to the playoffs. Jim Mora's first Saints team laid the foundation for a decade of winning like Saints fans had never seen before.

By late in the 1986 season, Mora's Saints began grabbing attention around the NFL for their work on the field. They were 6–5 through 11 games and were in the race for a playoff spot. The Saints went 1–4 the rest of the way. But progress had been made. The Saints would make a giant leap forward in 1987.

Louisiana native Bobby Hebert established himself as the starting quarterback that year. With Hebert and Mora, the Saints had their best season to date in 1987. The season

Quarterback Bobby Hebert led the Saints to the playoffs for the first time in 1987.

Linebacker Pat Swilling (56), the 1991 NFL Defensive Player of the Year, celebrates after tackling a Minnesota Vikings player in 1991.

was shortened from 16 to 15 games due to a players' strike. The regular players played in the first two games of the season before striking. After a week of no football, replacement players played three games.

The Saints were 3–2 at the end of the strike. They went 9–1 after that and finished 12–3 to make the playoffs for the first time.

THE DOME PATROL

During the late 1980s and early 1990s, the Saints featured one of the best sets of linebackers the NFL has ever seen. They were known as the Dome Patrol. Over the years the group included Rickey Jackson, Vaughan Johnson, Sam Mills, and Pat Swilling. The Dome Patrol helped lead New Orleans to its first winning season and playoff appearance in 1987.

From 1983 until 1991, the four players combined for 18 Pro Bowl selections. All four played together from 1986 until 1992. Swilling was named the NFL's Defensive Player of the Year in 1991. Jackson, however, was the biggest star. In 2010 he became the first player who spent most of his career with the Saints to be enshrined in the Pro Football Hall of Fame. During 13 years in New Orleans, Jackson amassed 115.0 sacks and seven interceptions.

The playoffs did not bring glory, however. New Orleans lost to the Minnesota Vikings 44–10 at the Superdome. Even with the loss, the 1987 season was a turning point for the Saints. The team made the playoffs four times in Mora's first seven seasons as coach. That included three straight years from 1990 to 1992. They also won their first division title in 1991. They went 11–5 to win the National Football Conference (NFC) West.

Mora's time as coach ended on a sour note during his eleventh season. He resigned after a 2–6 start in 1996. The Saints hired Hall of Famer Mike Ditka as their next head coach.

Rookie quarterback Aaron Brooks helped the Saints win a division title and their first playoff game in 2000.

Ditka had led the 1985 Chicago Bears to the Super Bowl XX title. But he could not reenergize the Saints.

Ditka was remembered for huge gamble in the 1999 NFL Draft. He traded all of the Saints' picks to Washington in exchange for the fifth overall selection. They used that pick to draft running back and Heisman Trophy winner Ricky Williams. Williams was a solid player, but most agree he was not worth all that Ditka gave up. Ditka was fired after the 1999 season with a 15–33 record in three seasons as the Saints' head coach.

Jim Haslett replaced Ditka. Haslett guided the Saints to a 10–6 record in 2000. It was their first playoff appearance since 1992. The Saints also won their second NFC West championship.

ONE OF THE GREATS

Willie Roaf never caught or threw a pass and he never scored a touchdown. But he was one of the greatest Saints of all time—and one of the best offensive tackles in NFL history. The 6-foot-5, 320-pounder was the Saints' first-round draft pick in 1993. Roaf started at tackle for them every year from 1993 to 2001. He was inducted into the Pro Football Hall of Fame in 2012.

The Saints had another first before the season was over: they won a playoff game. New Orleans took a 31–7 lead against the St. Louis Rams. But the defending Super Bowl champion Rams rallied in the fourth quarter. The Saints held on to win 31–28 at the Superdome. Wide receiver Willie Jackson had 142 receiving yards and three touchdowns to lead the Saints.

The Saints lost to the Vikings to end their season one week later. But they had reached a new milestone for the club.

CHAPTER 5

FROM TRAGEDY TO TRIUMPH

Life changed for the Saints and their fans in 2005. The team was preparing for a preseason game in Oakland. Back home, a devastating hurricane was on its way to New Orleans. Hurricane Katrina hit land on August 29. It caused massive flood damage and power loss to the Gulf Coast. The storm killed nearly 1,600 people. Thousands were left homeless. Eighty percent of the city was under water.

The Saints' home was also damaged. The hurricane tore a hole in the roof of the Superdome. Still, the stadium became a shelter for thousands of displaced residents.

The city began its long road to recovery. The Saints did, too. But they still had to play the 2005 season. The Saints played a preseason game in Oakland three days after the

Fans welcome the Saints to San Antonio, the team's temporary home after Hurricane Katrina hit New Orleans.

In 2006, the Saints drafted running back Reggie Bush, *left*, and signed quarterback Drew Brees to improve the offense.

hurricane made landfall. When it was over, they were unable to go back to New Orleans. Instead they flew to San Antonio, Texas. They would operate from San Antonio for the rest of the 2005 season.

The Saints played "home" games in three different locations that season away from New Orleans. Three games were at the Alamodome in San Antonio. Four were at Tiger Stadium in Baton Rouge, home of Louisiana State University. And the Saints' "home opener" was played against the New York Giants in the Giants' home stadium in New Jersey.

The Saints went into 2005 with playoff hopes. But the crazy schedule and distraction of the tragedy back home took a toll on the players. They finished 3–13 and won just once in their last 12 games.

The Saints went through several changes after that season. Coach Jim Haslett was fired and replaced by Sean Payton. The team also signed quarterback Drew Brees. He had started for the San Diego Chargers the previous four seasons. The Saints selected running back Reggie Bush in the first round of the 2006 NFL Draft. He had won the Heisman Trophy as college football's best player. All three would have a significant impact on the future of the Saints.

STEVE GLEASON

Steve Gleason was a Saints defensive back from 2000 to 2006. Fans remember him best for blocking a punt in the first game back in the Superdome after Hurricane Katrina. The team erected a statue of him making the play outside the Superdome. Gleason was diagnosed with ALS in 2011, a disease commonly known as Lou Gehrig's disease. Gleason stayed in contact with the Saints while battling the disease. He was so beloved that the team gave him a Super Bowl ring even though he didn't play on the 2009 team.

Some fans worried that the Saints would permanently relocate after Hurricane Katrina. But the team returned to the Superdome in 2006. The Saints went 10–6 and won the NFC South Division that season. They defeated the Philadelphia Eagles 27–24 in the playoffs. It was the second playoff win in team history.

The Saints then played in their first NFC Championship Game. The magic ended there. They lost to the Chicago Bears 39–14. The Saints went a combined 15–17 during the next two seasons before rising to new heights in 2009.

The Saints started 13–0 in 2009. They finished the regular season 13–3 and with the best record in the NFC. That earned them a bye in the first round of the playoffs. They beat the Arizona Cardinals 45–14 in the second round. Then they hosted the Minnesota Vikings in the NFC Championship Game.

New Orleans and Minnesota had been the dominant teams in the NFC all season. The Saints came out on top when they finally met. They won 31–28 in overtime to earn their first trip to the Super Bowl.

The Saints had been tremendous in the regular season. But many observers still favored the Indianapolis Colts in Super Bowl XLIV. The Colts had started the season 14–0, but they lost their final two games as many of their star players rested. The Colts came out strong and jumped to a 10–0 lead in Super Bowl XLIV. But two touchdown passes by Brees helped the Saints come back and take a 24–17 lead in the fourth quarter. Moments later, Saints cornerback Tracy Porter returned an

New Orleans Saints fans hold up signs to celebrate their team's 31–17 Super Bowl XLIV victory over the Indianapolis Colts.

interception 74 yards for a touchdown that wrapped up the Saints' 31–17 victory.

New Orleans is a city known for its partying on Mardi Gras. The Saints gave them another reason to party in February 2010. The fans had stuck by the team through decades of losing. After Hurricane Katrina, the Saints stuck with New Orleans and helped the residents stay positive during challenging times.

The Saints knew that winning the Super Bowl was not just about one game. It was about bringing pride to a team and a city that had suffered long enough.

CHAPTER 6

DREW'S DOMINANCE

Getting to the Super Bowl once is hard. Getting back there again is even harder. The Saints found that out in the 2010s. But with a quarterback like Drew Brees, they were always in the mix.

Brees led the Saints to winning records in 2010 and 2011. In 2011 they went 13–3 while Brees led the NFL in passing yards and touchdown passes. The Saints knocked off the Detroit Lions in the first round of the playoffs 45–28.

They met the San Francisco 49ers in the next round. The 49ers went up 17–0 early. But Brees threw two touchdown passes in the second quarter to make it 17–14 at halftime. Brees threw a 66-yard touchdown pass to tight end Jimmy Graham that gave the Saints a lead with 1:37 to go. But the

Drew Brees acknowledges Saints fans after he broke the NFL career passing yards record in 2018.

MARQUES COLSTON

Drew Brees has had success with many wide receivers in his career, none more so than Marques Colston. Colston was the last pick in the 2006 NFL Draft. He made a lot of teams regret skipping him. Colston was a rookie in Brees' first year in New Orleans. Over the next 10 seasons together, they formed a powerful partnership. Colston retired after the 2015 season as the Saints' all-time leader in catches, receiving yards, and touchdowns.

49ers came back to score with 17 seconds left and won 36–32.

As if that heartbreaker wasn't enough, the Saints got even worse news months later. The NFL had been investigating the team since 2010. The Saints were accused of paying bounties—illegal payments given to players who injure certain opponents. On March 2, 2012, the NFL announced that the Saints had been found guilty.

Not every Saints coach and player was a part of it. Brees denied knowing anything about it. But head coach Sean Payton was suspended for the entire 2012 season. Several other coaches and players faced shorter suspensions. The team was fined and forced to give up draft picks. Brees led the NFL in passing yards and touchdowns again that year. But the Saints went 7–9 and missed the playoffs. Payton returned the next year and the Saints bounced back. They went 11–5 and won a playoff game but lost in the second round.

Running back Alvin Kamara surpassed 1,500 yards from scrimmage in each of his first two NFL seasons.

Defense was the Saints' biggest problem in those years. From 2014 to 2016, the Saints ranked in the bottom five in the NFL in both points and yards allowed. They went 7–9 in each of those years.

In 2017 defensive coordinator Dennis Allen helped turn it around. The addition of NFL Defensive Rookie of the Year Marshon Lattimore at cornerback helped. And they still had an excellent offense. In addition to sturdy running back Mark Ingram, the Saints added the dynamic Alvin Kamara to the backfield. Kamara was the league's Offensive Rookie of the Year in 2017. They also had wide receiver Michael Thomas,

TB

Without Tom Benson, there might be no New Orleans Saints. Benson bought the Saints in 1985 when the team was rumored to be moving to Jacksonville, Florida. Instead, Benson kept the team in New Orleans, even through the tragedy of Hurricane Katrina. Born and raised in the city, Benson was always loyal to New Orleans. Benson died on March 15, 2018. The team honored him with a patch on their uniforms the following season.

who posted 1,000 or more receiving yards in each of his first three seasons.

The 2017 Saints won the NFC South but suffered a last-second loss at Minnesota in the playoffs. They improved to 13–3 in 2018, becoming a Super Bowl favorite. They beat the defending champion Philadelphia Eagles in their first playoff game. They then met the Los Angeles Rams in the conference title game with a chance to get back to the Super Bowl.

The Saints were at home in the Superdome. Their fans were loud and crazy as usual. The game was tied 20–20 late in the fourth quarter. The Saints had the ball and were driving. They were on the Rams 13-yard line.

On third down, Brees looked for receiver Tommylee Lewis. His pass was on target, but at the last second, Lewis was leveled by Rams cornerback Nickell Robey-Coleman. It appeared to be a pass interference penalty. But no call came.

In a controversial play, Saints receiver Tommylee Lewis (11) couldn't make the catch against the Rams' Nickell Robey-Coleman (23).

The penalty would have given the Saints a first down. They could have run the clock down and kicked a game-winning field goal on the last play of the game. Instead, the Rams had 1:41 remaining after the Saints kicked their field goal.

The Rams marched back down the field and tied the game with a field goal to force overtime. They went on to win and go to the Super Bowl. Saints fans were furious. But there was nothing they could do.

Saints fans had put up with a history of disappointment. The win in Super Bowl XLIV changed all that. But New Orleans fans were no less hungry to win another one.

TIMELINE

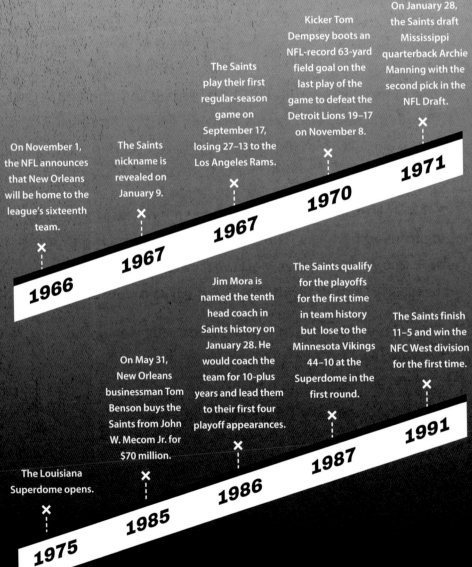

On November 1, the NFL announces that New Orleans will be home to the league's sixteenth team.

1966

The Saints nickname is revealed on January 9.

1967

The Saints play their first regular-season game on September 17, losing 27–13 to the Los Angeles Rams.

1967

Kicker Tom Dempsey boots an NFL-record 63-yard field goal on the last play of the game to defeat the Detroit Lions 19–17 on November 8.

1970

On January 28, the Saints draft Mississippi quarterback Archie Manning with the second pick in the NFL Draft.

1971

The Louisiana Superdome opens.

1975

On May 31, New Orleans businessman Tom Benson buys the Saints from John W. Mecom Jr. for $70 million.

1985

Jim Mora is named the tenth head coach in Saints history on January 28. He would coach the team for 10-plus years and lead them to their first four playoff appearances.

1986

The Saints qualify for the playoffs for the first time in team history but lose to the Minnesota Vikings 44–10 at the Superdome in the first round.

1987

The Saints finish 11–5 and win the NFC West division for the first time.

1991

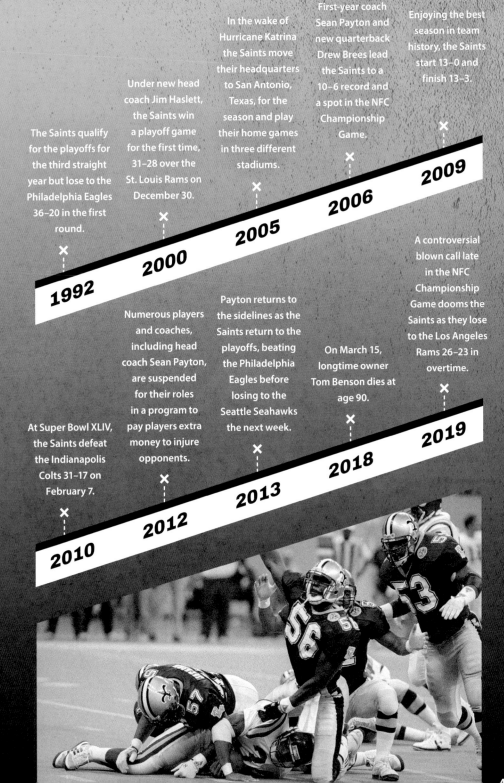

The Saints qualify for the playoffs for the third straight year but lose to the Philadelphia Eagles 36–20 in the first round.

1992

Under new head coach Jim Haslett, the Saints win a playoff game for the first time, 31–28 over the St. Louis Rams on December 30.

2000

In the wake of Hurricane Katrina the Saints move their headquarters to San Antonio, Texas, for the season and play their home games in three different stadiums.

2005

First-year coach Sean Payton and new quarterback Drew Brees lead the Saints to a 10–6 record and a spot in the NFC Championship Game.

2006

Enjoying the best season in team history, the Saints start 13–0 and finish 13–3.

2009

At Super Bowl XLIV, the Saints defeat the Indianapolis Colts 31–17 on February 7.

2010

Numerous players and coaches, including head coach Sean Payton, are suspended for their roles in a program to pay players extra money to injure opponents.

2012

Payton returns to the sidelines as the Saints return to the playoffs, beating the Philadelphia Eagles before losing to the Seattle Seahawks the next week.

2013

On March 15, longtime owner Tom Benson dies at age 90.

2018

A controversial blown call late in the NFC Championship Game dooms the Saints as they lose to the Los Angeles Rams 26–23 in overtime.

2019

QUICK STATS

FRANCHISE HISTORY

1967–

SUPER BOWLS
(wins in bold)

2009 (XLIV)

NFC CHAMPIONSHIP GAMES *(since 1970 AFL-NFL merger)*

2006, 2009, 2018

DIVISION CHAMPIONSHIPS *(since 1970 AFL-NFL merger)*

1991, 2000, 2006, 2009, 2011, 2017, 2018

KEY COACHES

Jim Haslett (2000–05): 45–51, 1–1 (playoffs)

Jim Mora (1986–96): 93–74, 0–4 (playoffs)

Sean Payton (2006–11, 2013–): 118–74, 8–6 (playoffs)

KEY PLAYERS
(position, seasons with team)

Morten Andersen (K, 1982–94)
Drew Brees (QB, 2006–)
Hoby Brenner (TE, 1981–93)
Stan Brock (T, 1980–92)
Marques Colston (WR, 2006–15)
Bobby Hebert (QB, 1985–89, 1991–92)
Dalton Hilliard (RB, 1986–93)
Joe Horn (WR, 2000–06)
Rickey Jackson (LB, 1981–93)
Vaughan Johnson (LB, 1986–93)
Archie Manning (QB, 1971–82)
Eric Martin (WR, 1985–93)
Deuce McAllister (RB, 2001–09)
Sam Mills (LB, 1986–94)
Derland Moore (DT, 1973–85)
William Roaf (T, 1993–2001)
George Rogers (RB, 1981–84)
Pat Swilling (LB, 1986–92)

HOME FIELDS

Superdome (1975–)
Tulane Stadium (1967–74)

*All statistics through 2018 season

QUOTES AND ANECDOTES

Bobby Hebert was the first quarterback to lead the Saints to the playoffs. It was fitting that he was the one to do it. Hebert was born in Cut Off, Louisiana, located about 65 miles (105 km) south of New Orleans. He starred at Northwestern State University in Natchitoches, Louisiana. He joined the Saints in 1985 and led them to the playoffs three times.

The United States Football League (USFL) wasn't around very long— just from 1983 to 1985. But it helped develop some of the best players and coaches in Saints history. Former head coach Jim Mora came to New Orleans from the USFL. Hebert and linebackers Vaughan Johnson and Sam Mills also starred in the USFL before coming to the Saints. Cornerback Antonio Gibson and running back Buford Jordan were among several other Saints who came from the USFL.

The Heisman Trophy is awarded every year to the top player in college football. Six Heisman Trophy winners have played for the Saints. They are running backs Reggie Bush, Earl Campbell, Mark Ingram, George Rogers, and Ricky Williams, and quarterback Danny Wuerffel. In addition, 1956 Heisman winner Paul Hornung was selected by the Saints in the 1967 expansion draft and participated in training camp, but he retired before the season and never played for the Saints.

Saints fans were incredibly upset about the blown call in the 2018 NFC Championship Game. The NFL even admitted that its officials had missed the call. But most fans weren't satisfied. Some even filed lawsuits in an attempt to convince the league to change the result of the game. Many Saints fans refused to watch the Super Bowl that year. The TV ratings for Super Bowl LIII were lower in New Orleans than in any other market in the country.

GLOSSARY

burden
An obligation that is difficult.

contract
An agreement to play for a certain team.

coordinator
An assistant coach who is in charge of the offense or defense.

cornerback
A defensive player who normally covers wide receivers.

defensive back
A cornerback or a safety, the defender who lines up the farthest from the ball and covers the opponent's receivers.

expansion
The addition of new teams to increase the size of a league.

franchise
A sports organization, including the top-level team and all minor league affiliates.

Hall of Fame
The highest honor a player or coach can get when his or her career is over.

Heisman Trophy
The award given yearly to the best player in college football.

overtime
An extra period of play when the score is tied after regulation.

replacement players
Players brought in while others are on strike.

strike
A work stoppage by employees in protest of working conditions.

tradition
Something that is handed down.

MORE INFORMATION

BOOKS

Cohn, Nate. *New Orleans Saints*. New York: AV2 by Weigl, 2018.

Ervin, Phil. *New Orleans Saints*. Minneapolis, MN: Abdo Publishing, 2017.

Graves, Will. *The Best NFL Offenses of All Time*. Minneapolis, MN: Abdo Publishing, 2014.

ONLINE RESOURCES

Booklinks
NONFICTION NETWORK
FREE! ONLINE NONFICTION RESOURCES

To learn more about the New Orleans Saints, visit **abdobooklinks.com** or scan this QR code. These links are routinely monitored and updated to provide the most current information available.

PLACE TO VISIT

New Orleans Saints Hall of Fame Museum
1500 Poydras St.
New Orleans, LA 70062
504–471–2192
saintshalloffame.com

This museum is home to exhibits and memorabilia representing the history of the New Orleans Saints. The museum is open by appointment only Monday through Friday.

INDEX

ABOUT THE AUTHOR

William Meier has worked as an author and editor in the publishing industry for more than 25 years. He resides in St. Louis, Missouri, with his wife and their poodle, Macy.